Edited by Nadirah Angail

In loving memory to my father and mother James and Louise Sessions who have been my biggest inspiration throughout my life. Your legacy continues to reign on this earth. I love you both forever!

Special recognition is given to Eric Matthews
for the I am **>** activity.

Special recognition is given to Tamika Rogers and Edward Oriowa for helping to develop the cover idea.

THANK YOU TO ALL FAMILY AND FRIENDS FOR THEIR SUPPORT WITH CREATING THIS BOOK.

CONTENTS

INTRODUCTION

This activity book was inspired by my granddaughter Charlie. As she entered puberty, I noticed her affect had grown flat and she lacked emotional drive. It bothered me that she was no longer positive, energetic and outgoing, so I spoke with her about her emotions surrounding the upcoming holidays. Instantly, Charlie's eyes lit up! She started smiling and was able to explain and verbalize her emotions.

THERE ARE OVER 40 MAJOR RELIGIOUS, CULTURAL, NATIONAL AND INFORMAL HOLIDAYS CELEBRATED IN THE UNITED STATES.

Holidays have a special way of bringing out joy, excitement and other specific feelings, so I knew I could use them in my clinical practice. Around Christmas 1995, when I was a new clinician in the school system and financially unable to purchase necessary therapeutic tools, I developed an activity called the Emotions Tree to bring out the emotions and creativity of my students and clients. The activity was a success, but it wasn't until 21 years later, when I began to use the tool with Charlie, that I further developed the concept into this book.

Parents, teachers, professionals and clinicians can use the Emotions Holiday Activity Book to develop emotional intelligence, which is the ability to identify, understand and manage one's own feelings as well as recognize the feelings of others. Through the Emotions Holiday Activity Book, children learn to be aware of their own feelings and explore those of others.

TO PARENTS

Please be as creative as you'd like while using these activities with your child. They were created to assist in eliciting the emotions that are most often suppressed by everyday life. Use these activities as prompts to open the door to necessary conversation.

TO TEACHERS, CLINICIANS AND OTHER PROFESSIONALS WORKING WITH CHILDREN

Please be creative and use these different activities as tools to unlock the emotions of your students or clients. It is recommended to start off by using the "I am >" tool as an introduction. Intellectually, cognitively, spiritually, physically, and mentally, we are all great—greater than the trials and life circumstances that weigh us down and inhibit our emotional expression. Take a moment to think, what are you greater (>) than? This activity along with the others will promote growth and unleash your students'/clients' emotions.

EMOTIONS

I AM
>

1. Brainstorm the meaning of the phrase, "I am greater than."

2. Write down at least three things you are greater than.

3. What are some of the problems bothering you in your life?

4. How do you resolve some of the problems bothering you in your life?

3

WHAT HOLIDAY AM I?

I am celebrated on the 1st day of the year. What am I?

_____

ASSOCIATED EMOTIONS AND/OR THEMES:

- ♥ Excitement
- ♥ Focus
- ♥ Reflection

                                       thejameslouisegroup@gmail.com

EMOTIONS

NEW

NEW YEAR'S DAY IS CELEBRATED ON JANUARY 1.

BEGINNING

ACTIVITY:

1. Does your family have any traditions for New Year's Eve or Day? Yes or No.

2. Set goals for the New Year.

3. How do you celebrate the New Year?

4. Does your family have any traditions that are celebrated for the New Year?

GOALS FOR NEW YEAR

_____

_____

_____

_____

Draw a picture of how you and your family celebrate the New Year:

WHAT HOLIDAY AM I?

I am celebrated on the 15th of January to honor a great man's nonviolent and valiant fight for civil rights. What am I?

_____

ASSOCIATED EMOTIONS AND/OR THEMES:

- ♥ Kindness
- ♥ Equality
- ♥ Consideration

EMOTIONS

DR. MARTIN LUTHER KING JR'S BIRTHDAY IS THE 15TH OF JANUARY

EQUALITY

9   thejameslouisegroup@gmail.com

ACTIVITY:

1. What types of dreams do you have?

2. What are some of your goals in life?

3. Do you think there should be equal rights for all Americans?

WRITE AT LEAST TWO OF YOUR DREAMS.

_____

_____

_____

WRITE AT LEAST TWO OF YOUR GOALS FOR THIS MONTH.

_____

_____

_____

_____

SHOULD ALL AMERICANS BE TREATED EQUALLY? EXPLAIN, WHY OR WHY NOT.

_____

_____

_____

_____

WHAT HOLIDAY AM I?

I am an informal holiday celebrated on January 24. My purpose is to encourage everyone to enjoy themselves and laugh!

_____

ASSOCIATED EMOTIONS AND/OR THEMES:

♥ Joy
♥ Laughter
♥ Fun

EMOTIONS

THIS HOLIDAY IS USUALLY HELD ON JANUARY 24 AND IT IS CALLED BELLY LAUGH DAY

LAUGHTER

Below draw a picture of yourself on Belly Laugh Day.

_____

_____

ACTIVITY:

1. Write a funny story or joke

See how many different words you can find in the words: BELLY LAUGH DAY

1. _____ 2. _____ 3. _____

4. _____ 5. _____ 6. _____

3. Practice laughing as loud as you can.

WHAT HOLIDAY AM I?

I am a holiday of love, celebrated on the 14th of February. What am I?

_____

ASSOCIATED EMOTIONS AND/OR THEMES:

- ♥ Love
- ♥ Affection
- ♥ Kindness

14   thejameslouisegroup@gmail.com

HEART OF

VALENTINE'S DAY IS CELEBRATED THE 14TH OF FEBRUARY

EMOTIONS

ACTIVITY:

- What does love mean to you?

- When was the last time you told someone you loved them? Be sure to tell someone today.

- Color the heart below and name some people you have shown love.

WHAT HOLIDAY AM I?

I am celebrated on the 3rd Monday in February to honor the leaders of the United States of America. What am I?

_____

ASSOCIATED EMOTIONS AND/OR THEMES:

- ♥ Leadership
- ♥ Power
- ♥ Patriotism

           thejameslouisegroup@gmail.com

PATRIOTIC

PRESIDENTS DAY IS CELEBRATED THE 3RD MONDAY IN FEBRUARY.

Color the picture below:

EMOTIONS

ACTIVITY:

WHO ARE YOUR FAVORITE PRESIDENTS?

_____

_____

_____

_____

IF YOU WERE THE PRESIDENT, WHAT WOULD YOU WANT TO LEAVE AS YOUR LEGACY?

_____

_____

_____

_____

WHY WOULD YOU WANT TO RULE THE COUNTRY?

_____

_____

_____

_____

WHAT HOLIDAY AM I?

I am celebrated in either March or April. I represent the resurrection of Jesus and often come with chocolate and bunnies. What am I?

_____

ASSOCIATED EMOTIONS AND/OR THEMES:

♥ Redemption
♥ Forgiveness

EMOTIONS EGGS

1. What fun ways do you celebrate Easter?

2. How does easter make you feel?

3. Decorate and color your egg.

 thejameslouisegroup@gmail.com

RESURRECTION

EMOTIONS

22 thejameslouisegroup@gmail.com

ACTIVITY:

1. What are your feelings about God?

2. Do you believe in God?

3. How are you respectful of others belief?

WRITE ABOUT YOUR FEELINGS OF GOD.

_____

_____

_____

_____

DO YOU BELIEVE IN GOD? WHY OR WHY NOT?

_____

_____

_____

_____

HOW ARE YOU RESPECTFUL TO OTHERS BELIEF?

_____

_____

_____

_____

WHAT HOLIDAY AM I?

I am celebrated the 1st of April and I'm full of pranks! What am I?

_____

ASSOCIATED EMOTIONS AND/OR THEMES:

- ♥ Joking
- ♥ Fun
- ♥ Silliness

FOOL'S EMOTIONS

1. How can you prank someone in a good way?

2. Name at least two things that someone did to you on April fool's day you never forgot?

3. Explain in the space below how this made you feel.

25

WHAT HOLIDAY AM I?

I am celebrated on April 22nd. I encourage others to protect our environment.
What am I?

_____

ASSOCIATED EMOTIONS AND/OR THEMES:

♥ Responsibility
♥ Creativity

26

thejameslouisegroup@gmail.com

EMOTIONS OF

EARTH

 thejameslouisegroup@gmail.com

ACTIVITY:

HOW CAN YOU KEEP THE AIR CLEAN?

_____

_____

_____

_____

HOW CAN YOU KEEP THE WATER CLEAN?

_____

_____

_____

_____

IF YOU SEE TRASH ON THE SIDE OF THE ROAD, WHAT ARE SOME THINGS YOU CAN DO TO HELP

CLEAN UP THE TRASH?

_____

_____

_____

_____

WHAT HOLIDAY AM I?

I am the 9th month of the Islamic calendar. I encourage people to avoid food and drink during the day. What am I?

_____

ASSOCIATED EMOTIONS AND/OR THEMES:

♥ Discipline
♥ Self-Control
♥ Internal Strength

       thejameslouisegroup@gmail.com

EMOTIONS

RAMADAN IS CELEBRATED BY MUSLIMS FOR 29 OR 30 DAYS. IT IS THE NAME OF THE ISLAMIC CALENDAR'S NINTH MONTH.

DURING RAMADAN, MUSLIMS OBSERVE THE FAST OF RAMADAN FROM DAWN TO SUNSET. THEY DO NOT EAT OR DRINK DURING THAT TIME. THIS IS A TIME TO FOCUS ON YOUR INNER SELF.

WRITE A STORY OF HOW YOU PLAN TO FOCUS ON YOURSELF AND YOUR ABILITIES.

RAMADAN

thejameslouisegroup@gmail.com

ACTIVITY:

IS THE ISLAMIC CALENDAR A SOLAR OR LUNAR CALENDAR?

_____

_____

IN THE MUSLIM CALENDAR, DOES THE HOLIDAY BEGIN ON THE SUNSET OF THE PREVIOUS DAY?

_____

WHEN IS THE LAST TIME THAT YOU FASTED?

_____

_____

HAVE YOU EVER FASTED? IF SO, WRITE ABOUT YOUR LAST EXPERIENCE.

WHAT HOLIDAY AM I?

I am celebrated on the 2nd Sunday in May. Mothers love me! What am I?

_____

ASSOCIATED EMOTIONS AND/OR THEMES:

♥ Love
♥ Appreciation

 thejameslouisegroup@gmail.com

EMOTIONS

MOTHER'S DAY IS CELEBRATED ON THE 2ND SUNDAY IN MAY.

Draw a picture of your mother:

MOTHER

ACTIVITY:

WHAT IS THE ROLE OF YOUR MOTHER?

_____

_____

_____

HOW DO YOU FEEL ABOUT YOUR MOTHER?

_____

_____

_____

HOW DOES YOUR MOTHER MAKE YOU FEEL?

_____

_____

_____

WHAT DO YOU LOVE THE MOST ABOUT YOUR MOTHER?

_____

_____

_____

HOW DOES YOUR MOTHER CARE FOR YOU? WHAT DOES SHE DO TO TAKE CARE OF YOU?

_____

_____

_____

WHAT HOLIDAY AM I?

My purpose is to honor veterans who have passed. I am celebrated on the last Monday in May. What am I?

_____

ASSOCIATED EMOTIONS AND/OR THEMES:

- ♥ Remembrance
- ♥ Honor
- ♥ Respect

thejameslouisegroup@gmail.com

EMOTIONS

Memorial Day honors veterans, which is celebrated on the last Monday in May.
Draw a picture of someone that you honor.

REMEMBRANCE

36 thejameslouisegroup@gmail.com

ACTIVITY:

1. Who in your life can you honor?

2. Take time out to remember a family member, friend or pet that has died.

3. Do something kind for a veteran that you know.

WRITE DOWN THE NAMES OF SOME PEOPLE THAT YOU CAN HONOR.

_____

_____

_____

NAME A FAMILY MEMBER, FRIEND OR PET THAT HAS DIED. HOW CAN YOU SHOW HONOR?

_____

_____

_____

WHAT CAN YOU DO FOR A VETERAN THAT YOU KNOW?

_____

_____

_____

WHAT HOLIDAY AM I?

I am celebrated on the 3rd Sunday in June. I encourage people to show love to their fathers. What am I?

_____

ASSOCIATED EMOTIONS AND/OR THEMES:

♥ Love
♥ Appreciation

 thejameslouisegroup@gmail.com

EMOTIONS

FATHER'S DAY IS CELEBRATED THE 3RD SUNDAY IN JUNE.

Draw a picture of your father.

FATHER

 thejameslouisegroup@gmail.com

ACTIVITY:

1. What is the role of your father?

2. How do you feel about your father?

3. How does your father make you feel?

WHAT DO YOU LOVE MOST ABOUT YOUR FATHER?

_____

_____

_____

NAME SOMETHING SPECIAL THAT YOU DO WITH YOUR FATHER OR WOULD LIKE TO DO.

_____

_____

_____

     thejameslouisegroup@gmail.com

WHAT HOLIDAY AM I?

I am celebrated to mark the birthday of America. Lots of fireworks are involved.
What am I?

_____

ASSOCIATED EMOTIONS AND/OR THEMES:

- ♥ Independence
- ♥ Self-Control
- ♥ Internal Strength

EMOTIONS

INDEPENDENCE DAY IS CELEBRATED ON JULY 4TH

Draw something that makes you feel excited

FIREWORKS

ACTIVITY:

1. Why do Americans celebrate the 4th of July?

2. What makes you feel independent?

3. What makes you feel excited?

WRITE DOWN WHY AMERICANS CELEBRATE THE 4TH OF JULY.

_____

_____

_____

WHAT ARE AT LEAST THREE THINGS THAT MAKE YOU FEEL INDEPENDENT?

_____

_____

_____

WHAT ARE AT LEAST THREE THINGS THAT MAKE YOU FEEL EXCITED?

_____

_____

_____

WHAT HOLIDAY AM I?

I am celebrated on the 1st Monday in September. I was created to honor those in the labor movement. What am I?

_____

ASSOCIATED EMOTIONS AND/OR THEMES:

- ♥ Hard work
- ♥ Balance
- ♥ Relaxation

thejameslouisegroup@gmail.com

EMOTIONS

Draw a picture of how you take a break from stressors in your life:

BREAK

thejameslouisegroup@gmail.com

ACTIVITY:

1. Don't allow yourself to get upset about anything today.

2. Talk about how taking a break from an explosive emotion can make you feel better.

3. Take time out to meditate on today.

WHAT HOLIDAY AM I?

I am celebrated on the 31st of October. I come with lots of tricks and treats.
What am I?

_____

ASSOCIATED EMOTIONS AND/OR THEMES:

♥ Fun
♥ Make-believe
♥ Imagination

47 thejameslouisegroup@gmail.com

EMOTIONS

HALLOWEEN IS CELEBRATED THE 31ST OF OCTOBER

Decorate your Jack o Lantern.

PUMPKINS

thejameslouisegroup@gmail.com

ACTIVITY:

1. What is Halloween?

2. How do you feel about Halloween?

3. Name a trick or treat that you have done to others.

WHAT DOES HALLOWEEN MEAN TO YOU?

_____

_____

_____

WHAT DO YOU LIKE MOST ABOUT HALLOWEEN?

_____

_____

_____

WHAT IS SOMETHING YOU HAVE DONE THAT WAS EITHER A TRICK OR A TREAT TO SOMEONE ELSE?

_____

_____

_____

WHAT HOLIDAY AM I?

I am celebrated on November 11th, to honor veterans who have served.
What am I?

_____

ASSOCIATED EMOTIONS AND/OR THEMES:

- ♥ Respect
- ♥ Honor
- ♥ Tradition
- ♥ Service

50   thejameslouisegroup@gmail.com

EMOTIONS OF

VETERANS DAY IS CELEBRATED FOR THE SERVICES OF VETERANS. IF YOU SEE A VETERAN ON TODAY, SALUTE THEM, SAY SOMETHING KIND OR DO A KIND GESTURE.

SERVICES

thejameslouisegroup@gmail.com

ACTIVITY:

Draw a picture of something you could do to serve others:

Do you participate in any type of community service program? If not, can you think of one you could join?

List some services you could do for friends or classmates.

Perform a random act of kindness every month.

WHAT HOLIDAY AM I?

I am celebrated on the 4th Thursday in November.
I remind everyone to be thankful. What am I?

_____

ASSOCIATED EMOTIONS AND/OR THEMES:

♥ Gratitude
♥ Togetherness
♥ Family

                    thejameslouisegroup@gmail.com

EMOTIONS

THANKSGIVING IS CELEBRATED THE 4TH THURSDAY IN NOVEMBER

COLOR THE TURKEY BELOW

THANKS

ACTIVITY:

1. How do you celebrate Thanksgiving?

2. Do you think Thanksgiving is a time for family?

3. How do you feel about having to spend Thanksgiving away from a family member?

WRITE DOWN THE REASON WE CELEBRATE THANKSGIVING

_____

_____

_____

_____

WRITE DOWN WHY YOU THINK THANKSGIVING IS A TIME TO SPEND OR NOT SPEND WITH FAMILY

_____

_____

_____

_____

WRITE DOWN HOW YOU WOULD FEEL IF YOUR THANKSGIVING DAY HAD TO BE SPLIT BETWEEN PARENTS

_____

_____

_____

_____

 thejameslouisegroup@gmail.com

WHAT HOLIDAY AM I?

I am celebrated on the 25th day of December to commemorate the birth of Jesus.
What am I?

_____

ASSOCIATED EMOTIONS AND/OR THEMES:

- ♥ Forgiveness
- ♥ Kindness
- ♥ Love

                                       thejameslouisegroup@gmail.com

EMOTIONS

DECORATE THE CHRISTMAS TREE AND BE AS CREATIVE AS YOU WOULD LIKE. DRAW ORNAMENTS, CANDY CANES, BULBS ETC. THE TREE DOES NOT HAVE TO BE COLORED GREEN. YOU CAN USE ANY COLOR.

TREE

thejameslouisegroup@gmail.com

ACTIVITY:

1. DO YOU THINK EVERYONE IS HAPPY AROUND CHRISTMAS? WHY OR WHY NOT?

_____

_____

_____

_____

2. NAME AT LEAST TWO THINGS YOU ARE GRATEFUL FOR IN YOUR LIFE.

_____

_____

_____

_____

_____

3. WHAT IS SOMETHING YOU CAN DO TO MAKE SOMEONE ELSE FEEL SPECIAL ON CHRISTMAS?

_____

_____

_____

As a bonus make something special for a loved one!!!!!

WHAT HOLIDAY AM I?

I am a Jewish holiday that begins in America on December 25th. I honor the rededication of the Temple of Jerusalem. What am I?

_____

ASSOCIATED EMOTIONS AND/OR THEMES:

- ♥ Heritage
- ♥ History
- ♥ Faith

EMOTIONS

HANUKKAH IS AN 8-DAY-LONG CELEBRATION. IT BEGINS IN THE US ON DECEMBER 25TH AND IS THE JEWISH FESTIVAL OF LIGHTS IN REMEMBRANCE OF THE REDEDICATION OF THE TEMPLE IN JERUSALEM.

HANUKKAH

1. What kind of community service can you think of?

2. During this month, try to provide a service to someone else, (i.e.) friend/ classmate.

3. Perform a Random Act of Kindness.

ACTIVITY:

THE NINTH CANDLE USED IN THE JEWISH FESTIVAL DURING HANUKKAH AS A HELPER.
Describe how you can be a helper to someone else.
Write your answers in the candles.

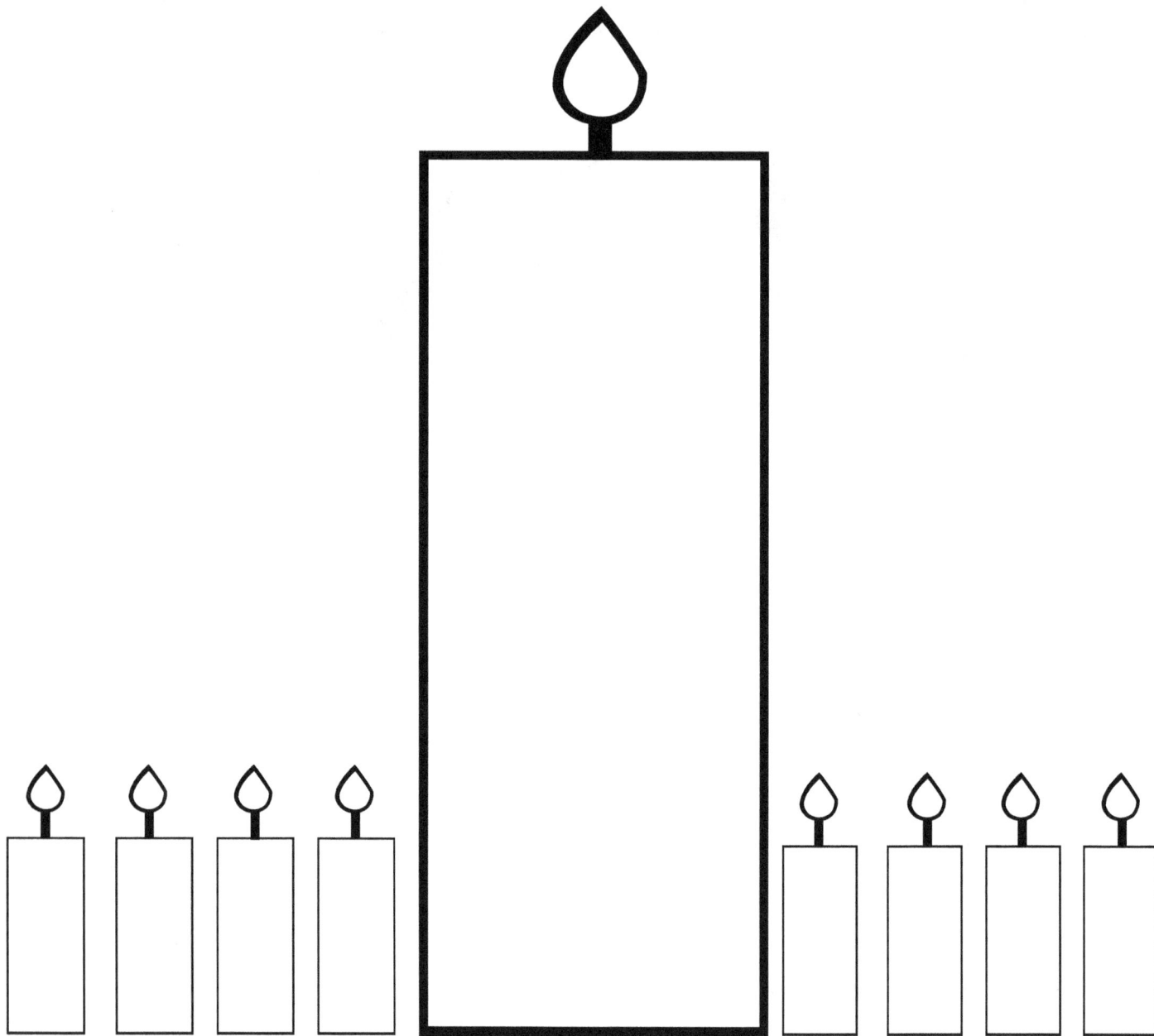

WHAT HOLIDAY AM I?

I am a seven-day celebration that begins on December 26th. There are seven principles associated with the holiday. What am I?

_____

ASSOCIATED EMOTIONS AND/OR THEMES:

- ♥ Culture
- ♥ Unity
- ♥ History
- ♥ Pride

EMOTIONS

KWANZAA IS AN AFRICAN AMERICAN HOLIDAY CELEBRATED FROM DECEMBER 26-JANUARY 1. THERE ARE SEVEN PRINCIPLES ASSOCIATED WITH THE HOLIDAY AND EACH DAY FOCUSES ON A CORE VALUE OF UNITY, SELF-DETERMINATION, COLLECTIVE WORK AND RESPONSIBILITY, COOPERATIVE ECONOMICS, PURPOSE, CREATIVITY, AND FAITH.

HERITAGE

ACTIVITY:

1. What are some of your core values?

2. What are the colors of Kwanzaa?

3. When is the last time that you gave someone a gift?

1. What do the three candles on the left represent_____

2. What dot the three candles on the right represent_____

3. What does the black candle in the middle represent_____

BELOW WRITE YOUR OWN WORD FOR EACH LETTER.

S   A   H
T   F   O
R   R   P
U   I   E
G   C
G
L
E

                thejameslouisegroup@gmail.com